What is a Family?
a question & answer book

Tamia Sheldon

xist Publishing

What makes a family? Lets think about what a family is.
This family loves to cuddle up together and read books.
What books do you like to read?

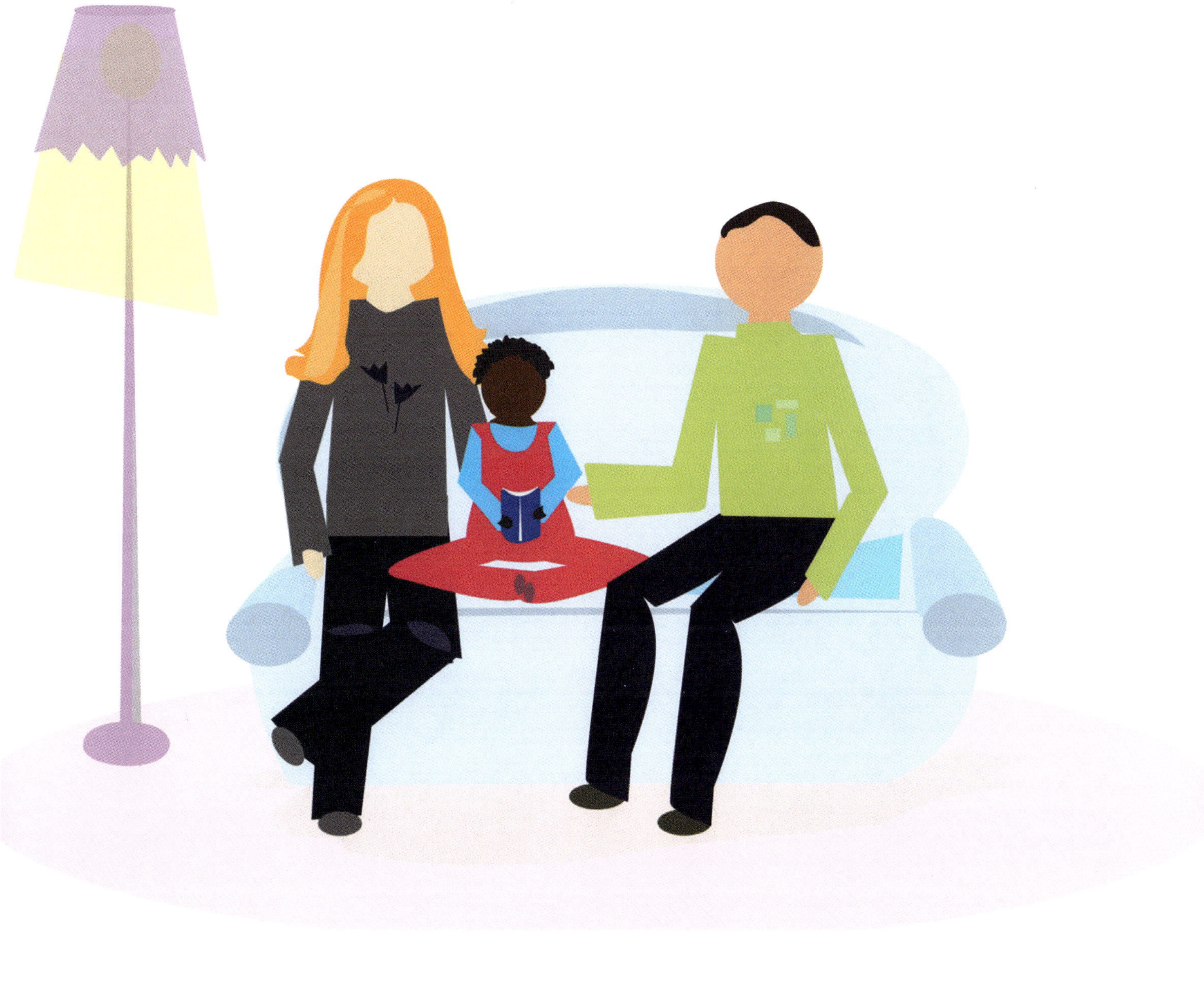

This family is moving!
Has your family ever moved to a new home?

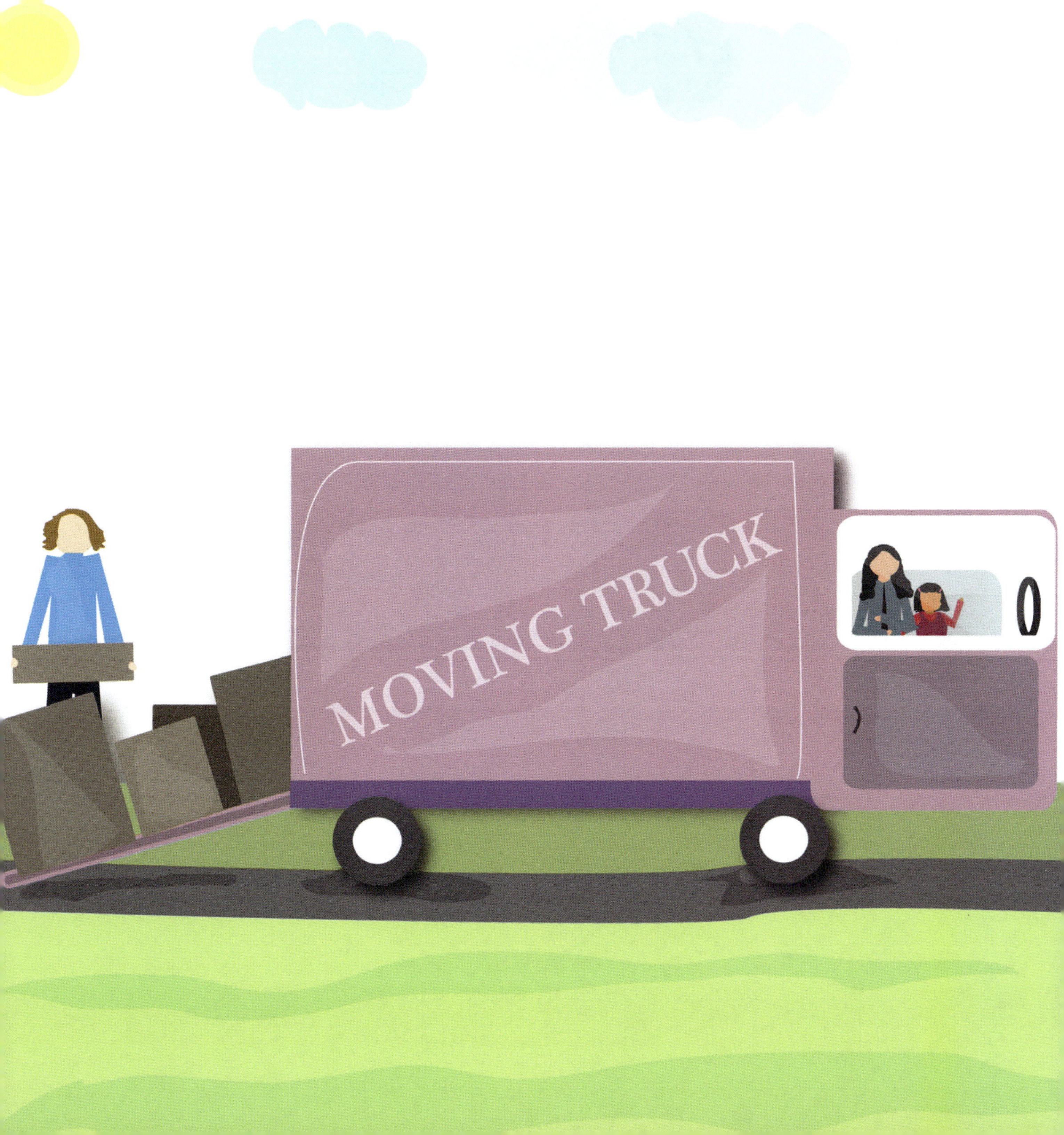
MOVING TRUCK

Some families are musical and love to sing.
This family has a family band and plays music together.
Does your family like to sing or play music?

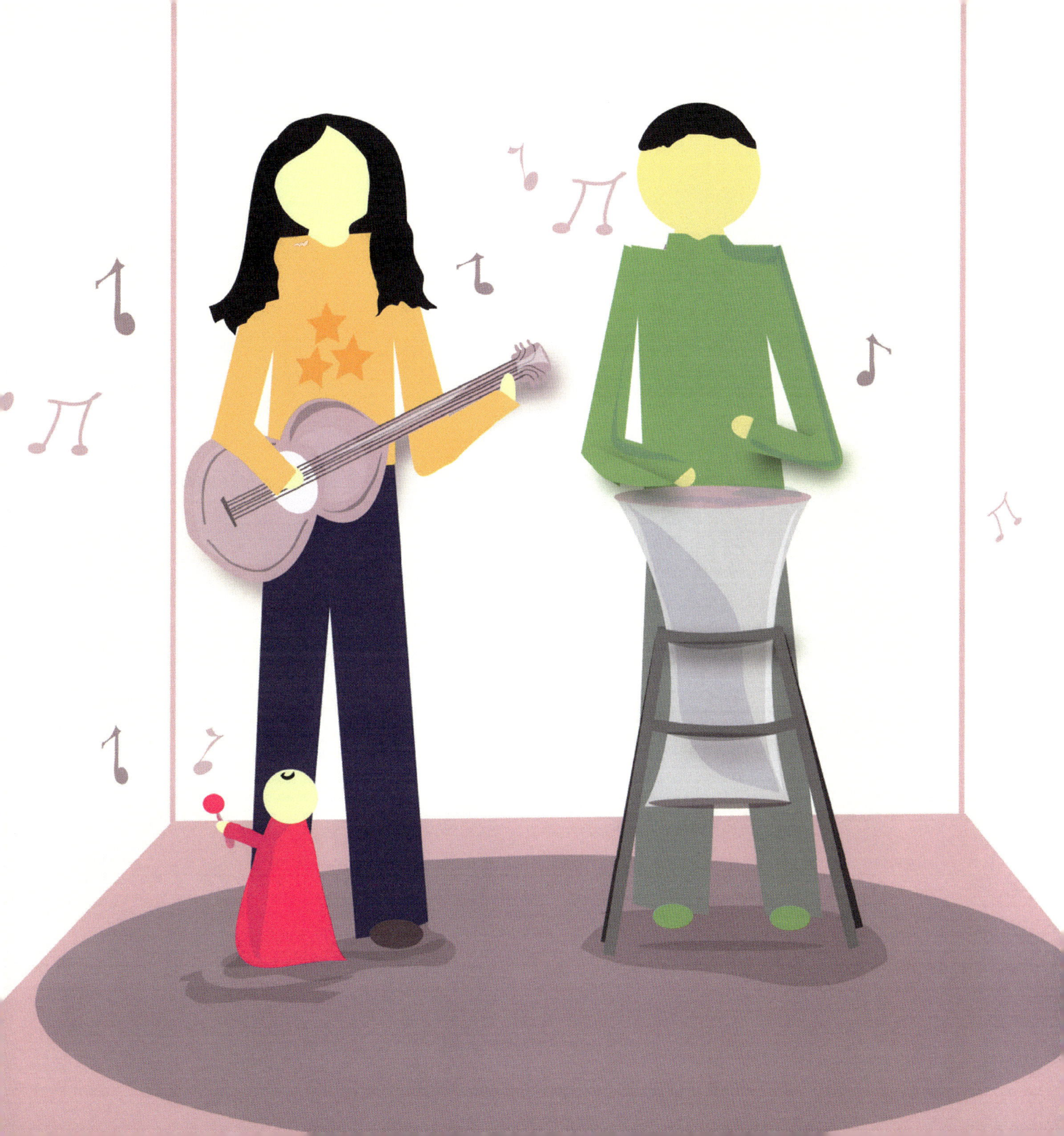

This family loves to cook together—
they like to make pizza and toss the dough!
What kinds of food does your family like?

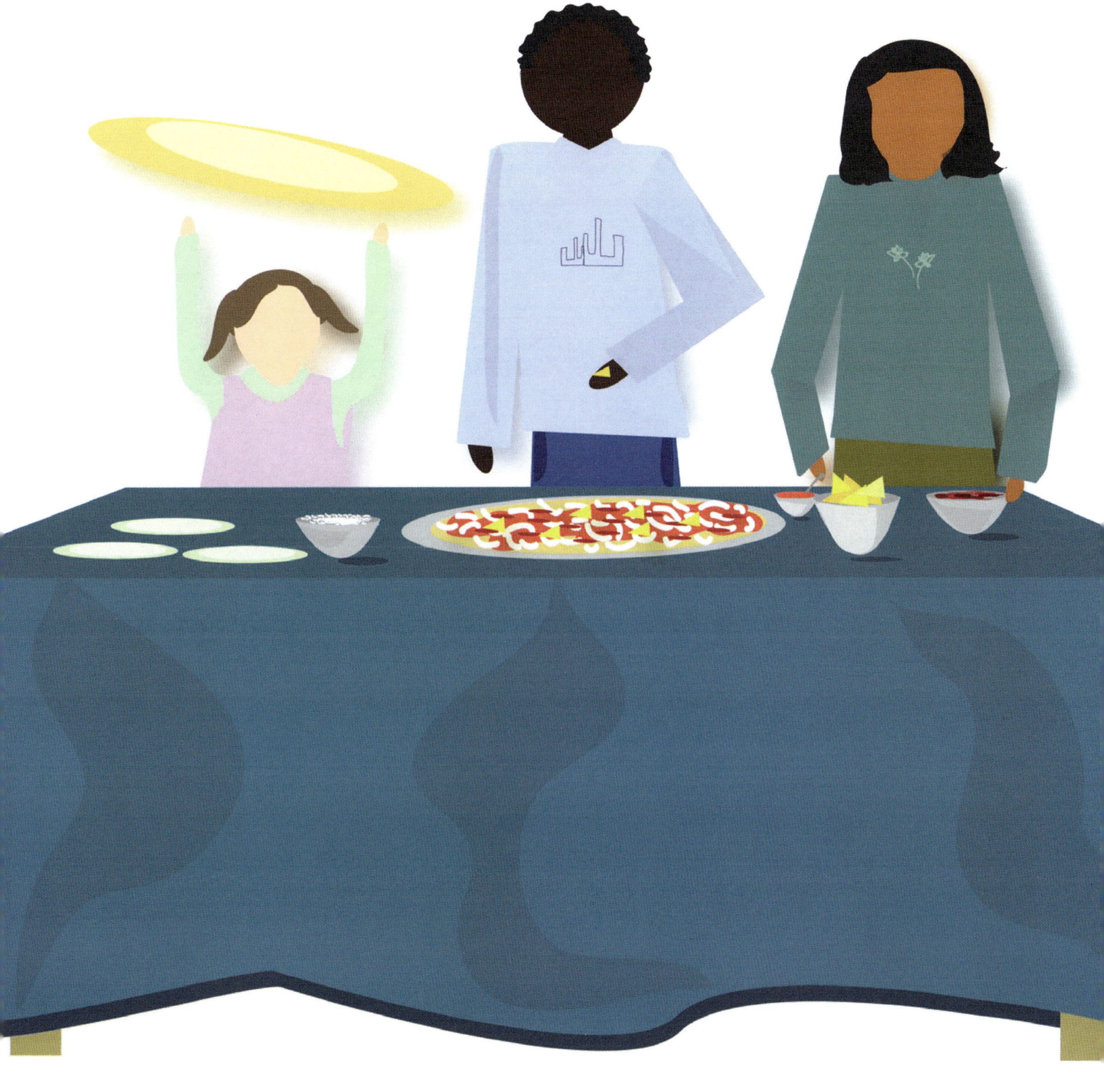

This family is going on a vacation!
Has your family ever taken a trip together?
Where did you go?

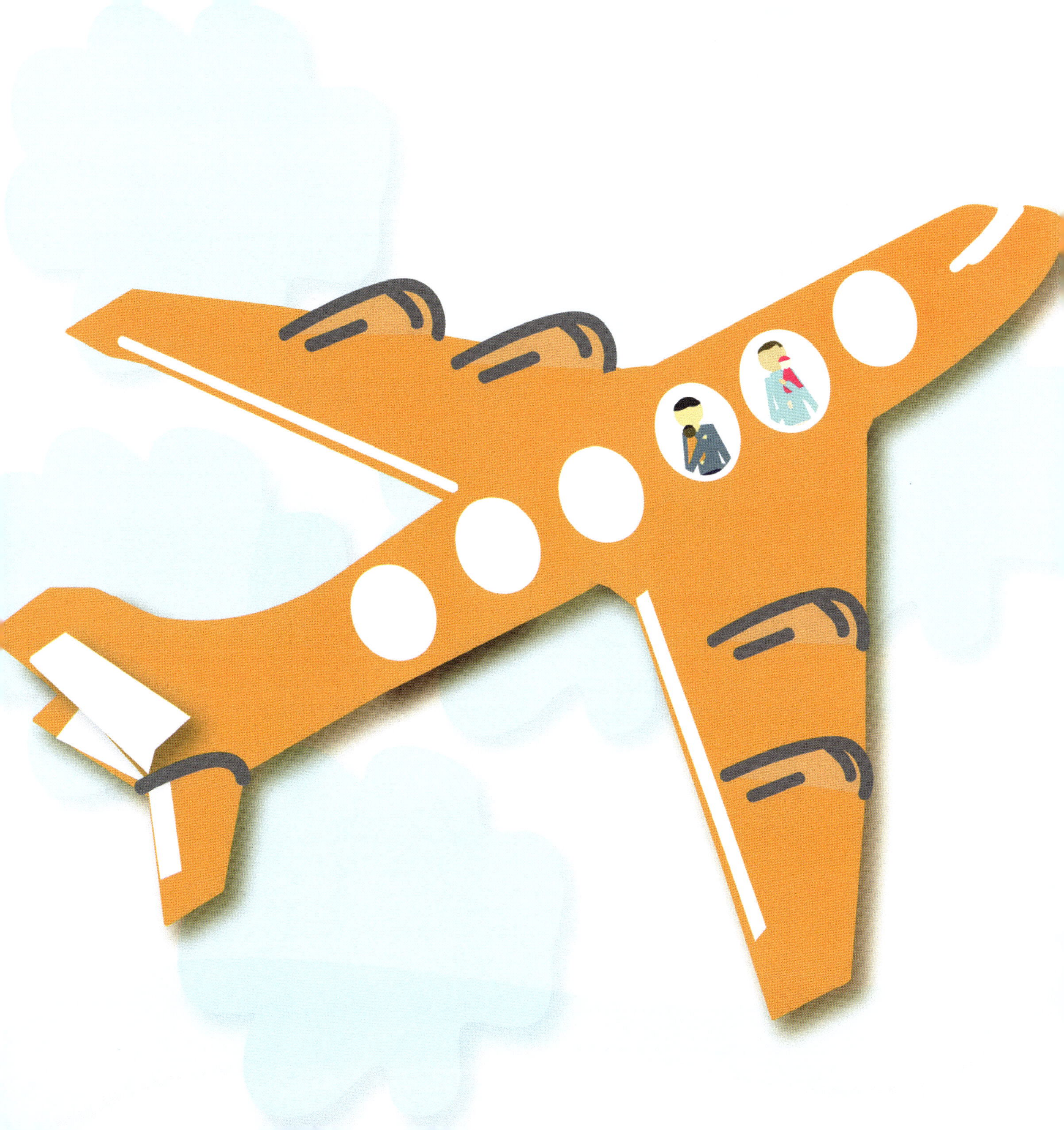

This family loves to dance.
Does your family like dancing?

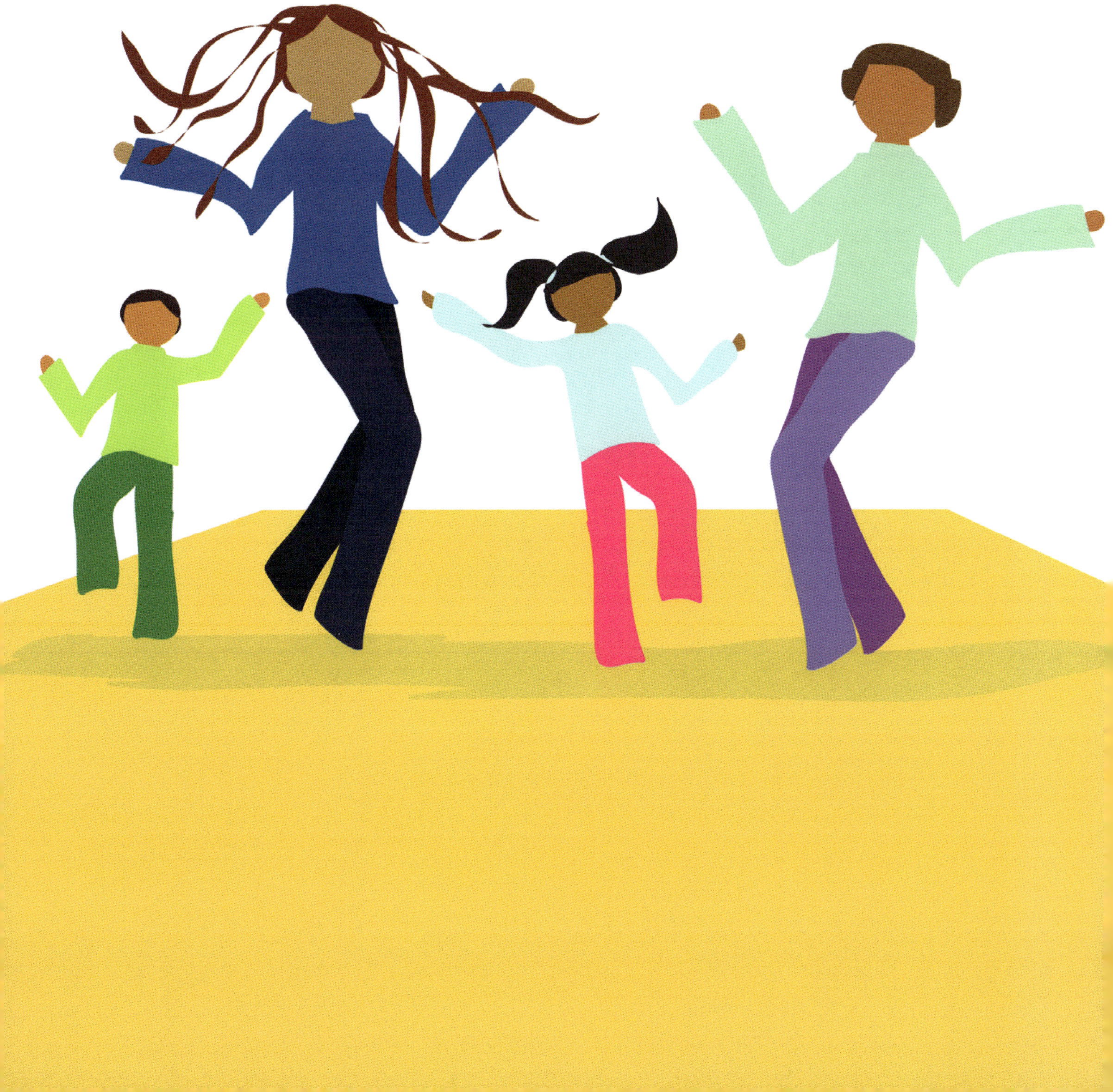

When family members get hurt or sick
we take care of them and make them feel better.
Have you ever been really sick?

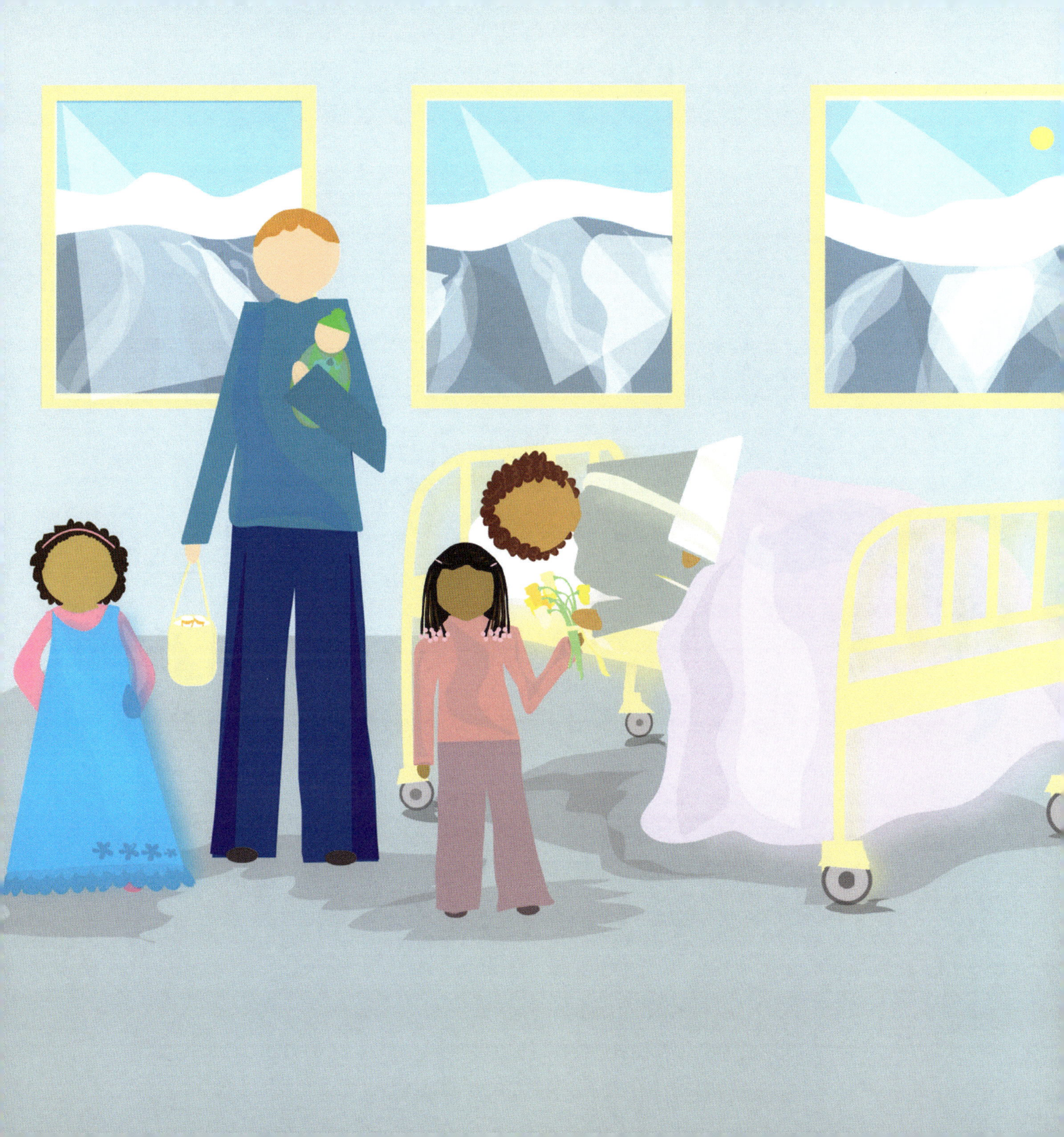

Families do chores together.
Does your family work together to keep your home clean?
What kind of chores do you do?

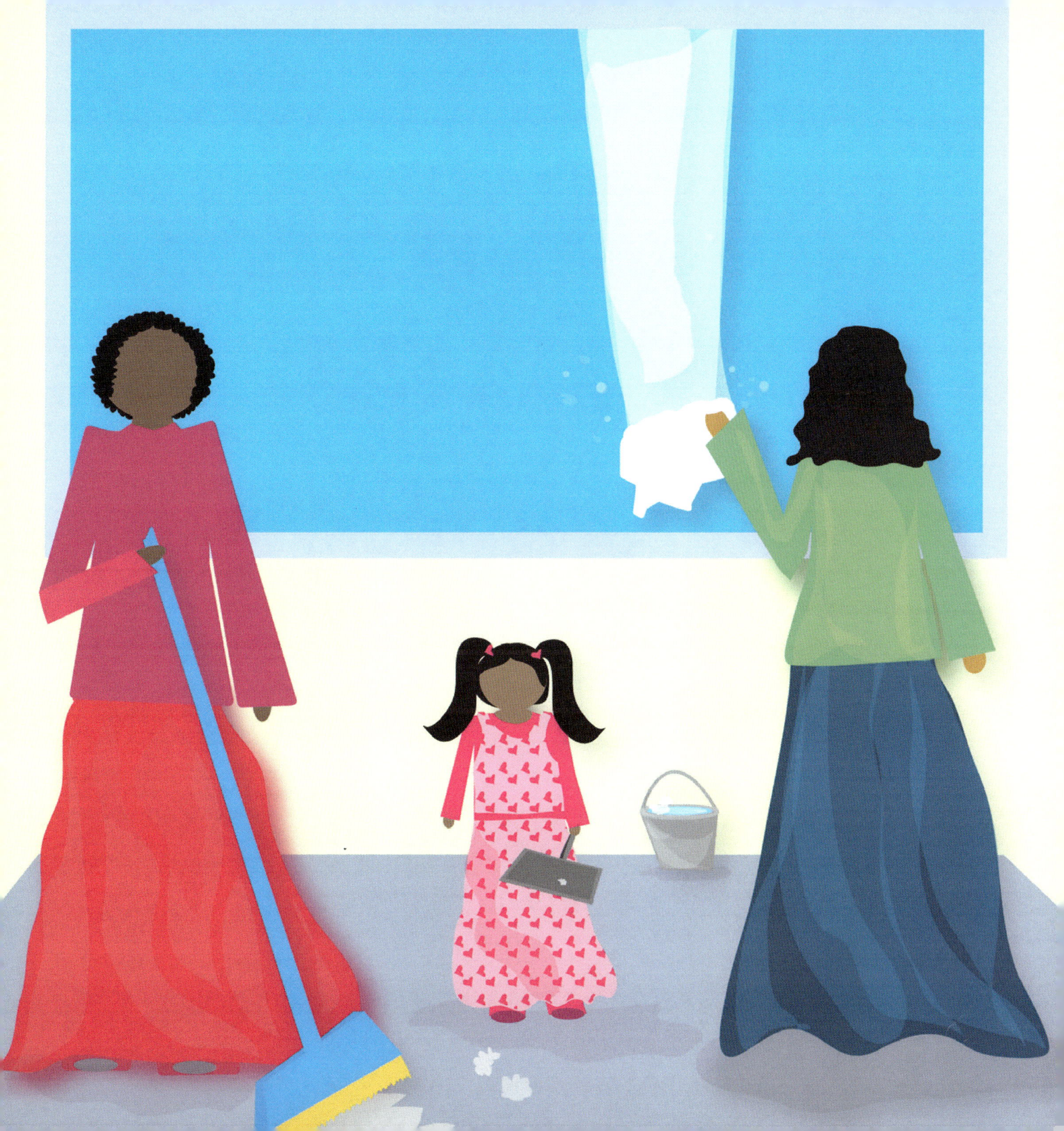

Some families go to the playground and play together.
Has your family every played at a park?
What was your favorite part?

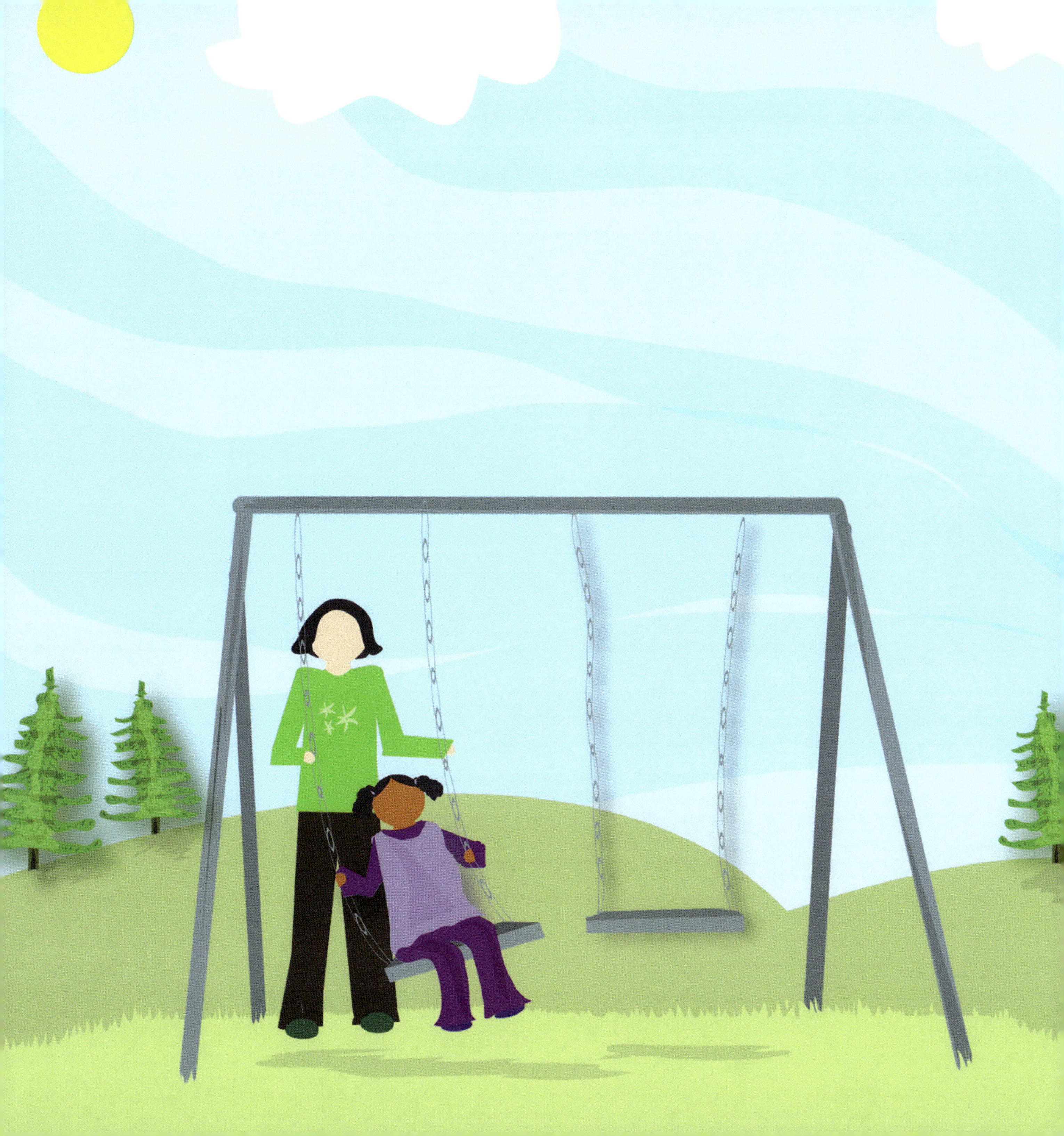

Families often live together in a house or apartment.
What kind of home do you live in?

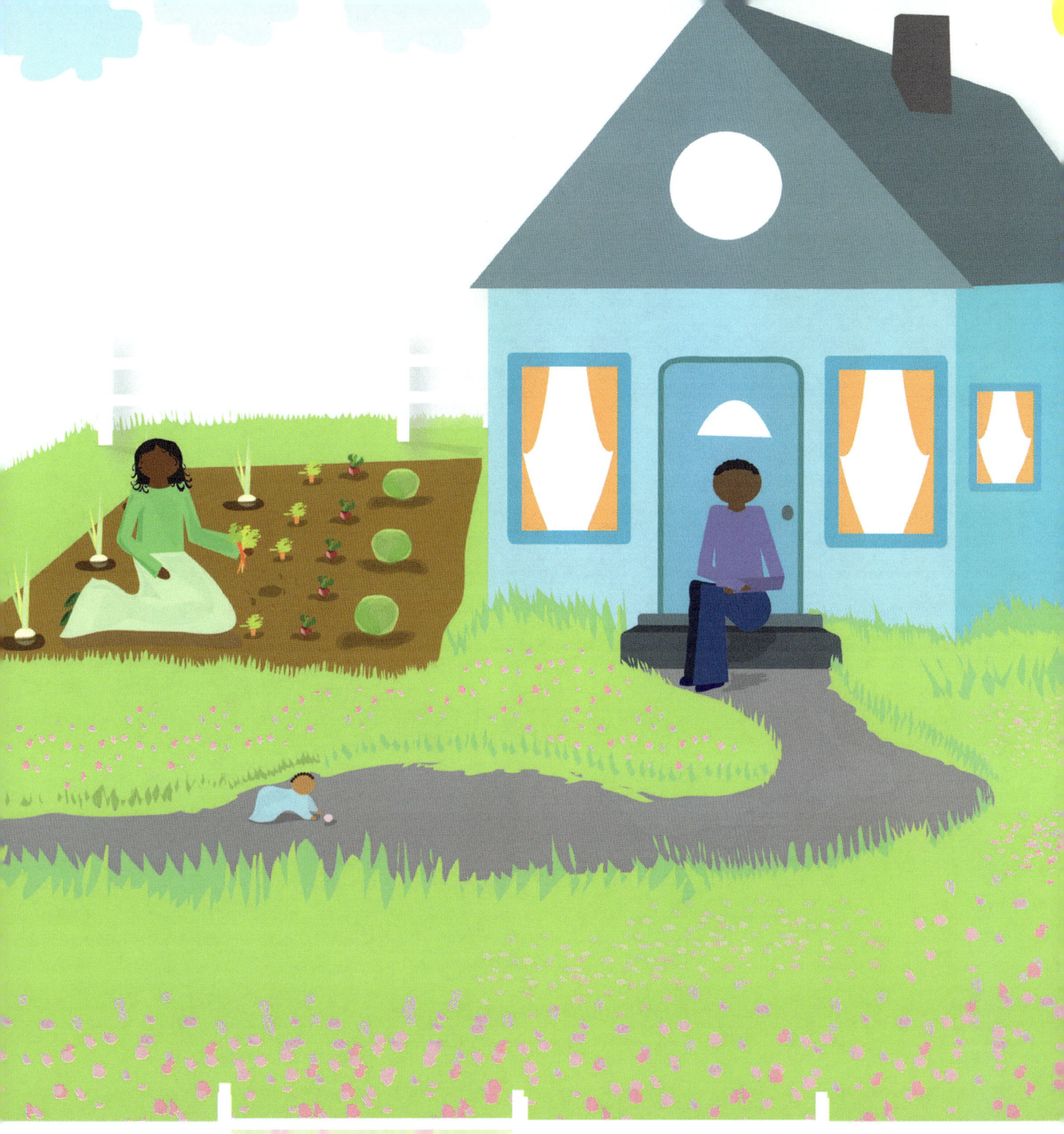

Some families like to have fun playing sports together.
This family loves to play soccer.
Which sports does your family play?

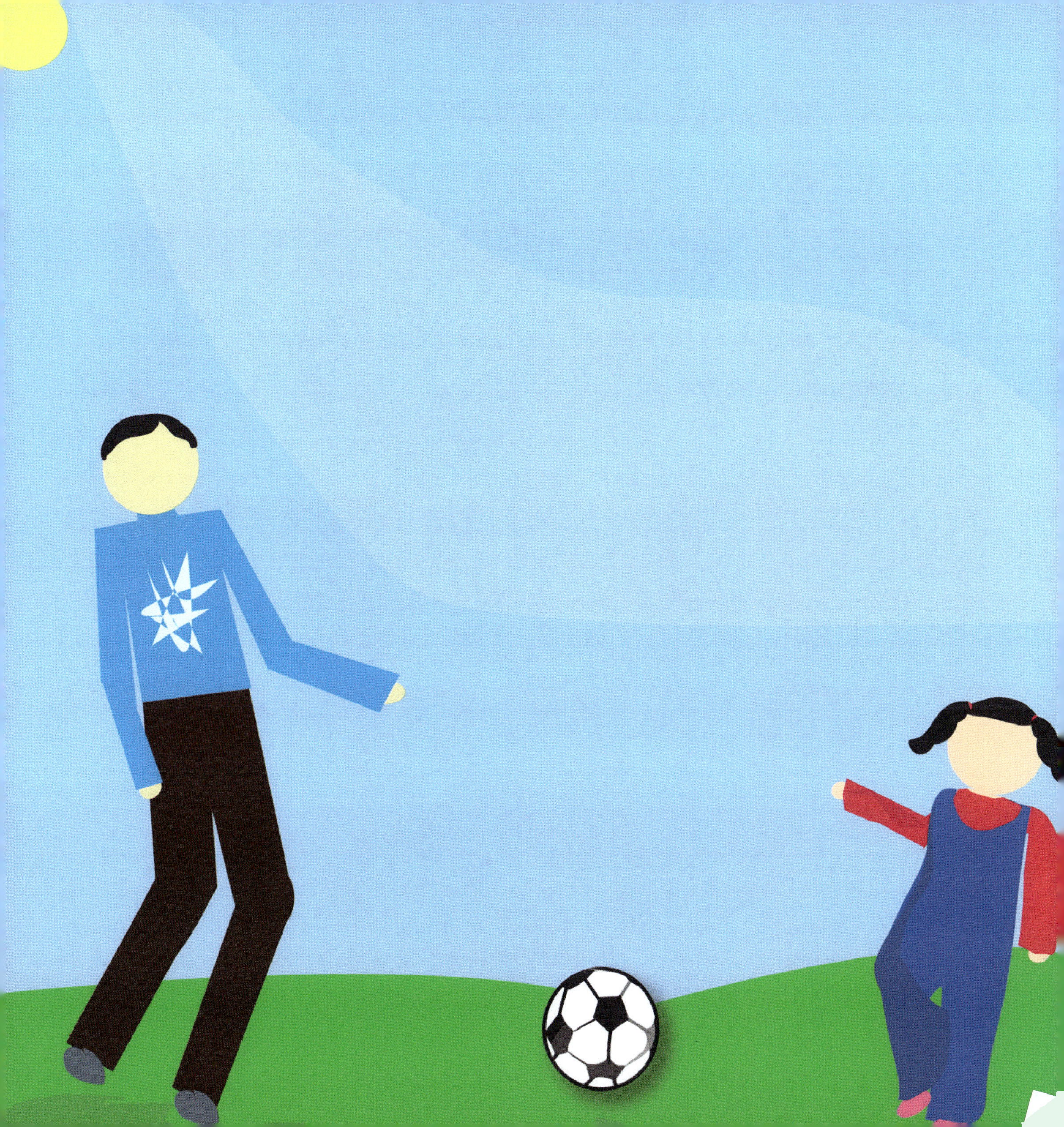

Some families are small and others are larger.
This family has many people living together.
How many people are in your family?

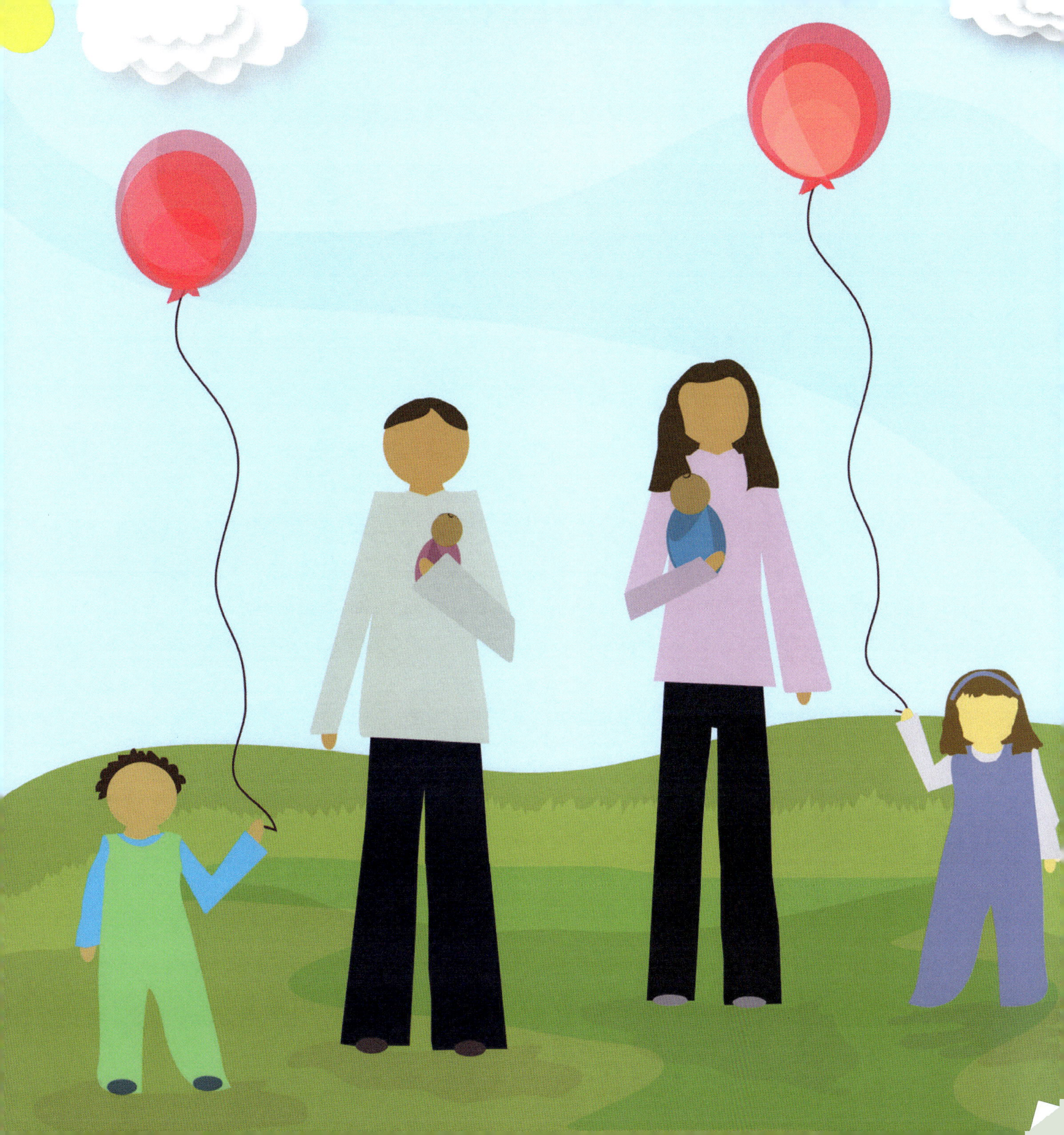

This family loves to go shopping together.
Does your family shop together?
What do you like to buy?

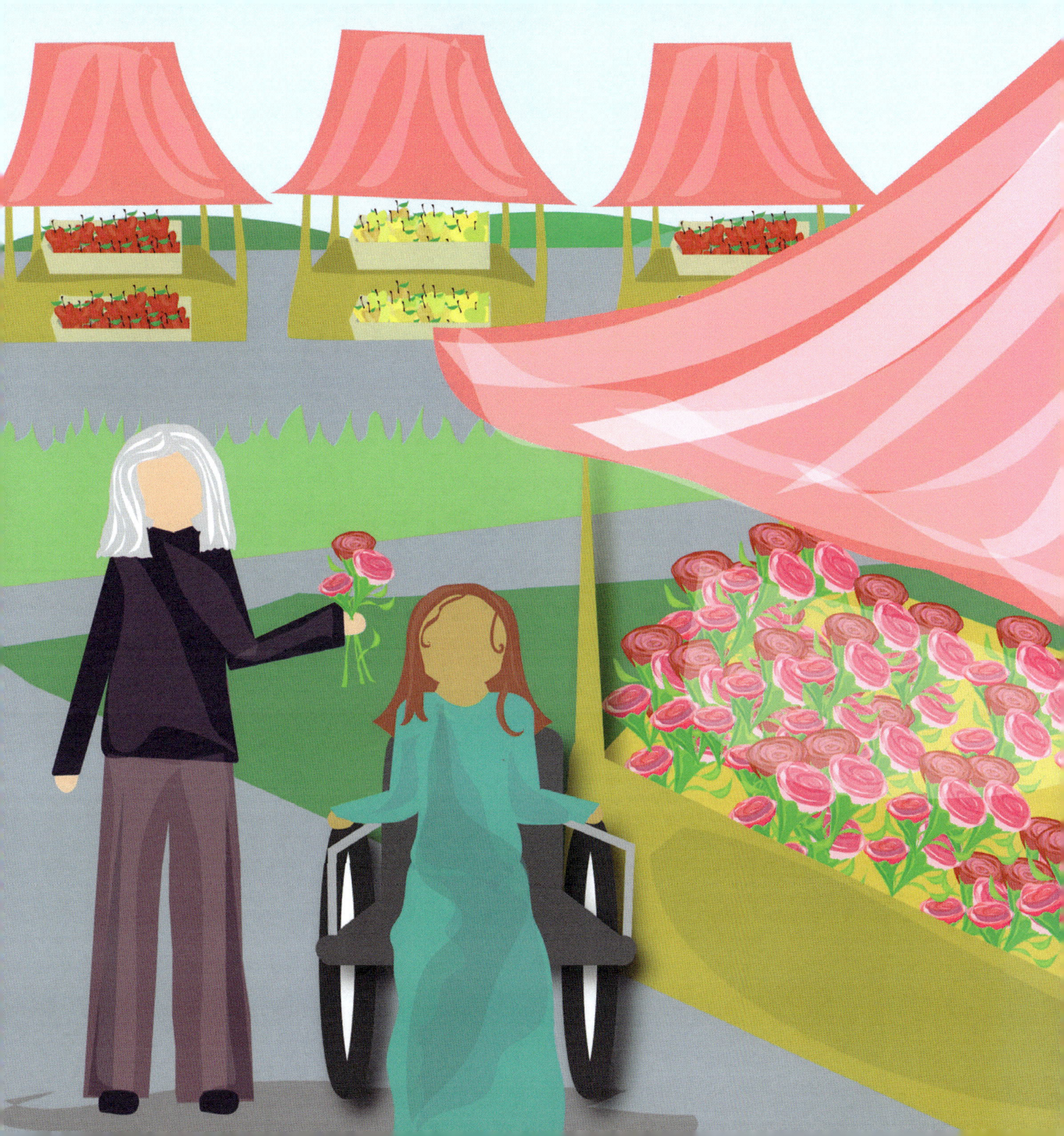

This family lives far apart from each other,
but they keep in touch by talking on the phone.
Do you talk to your family on the phone?

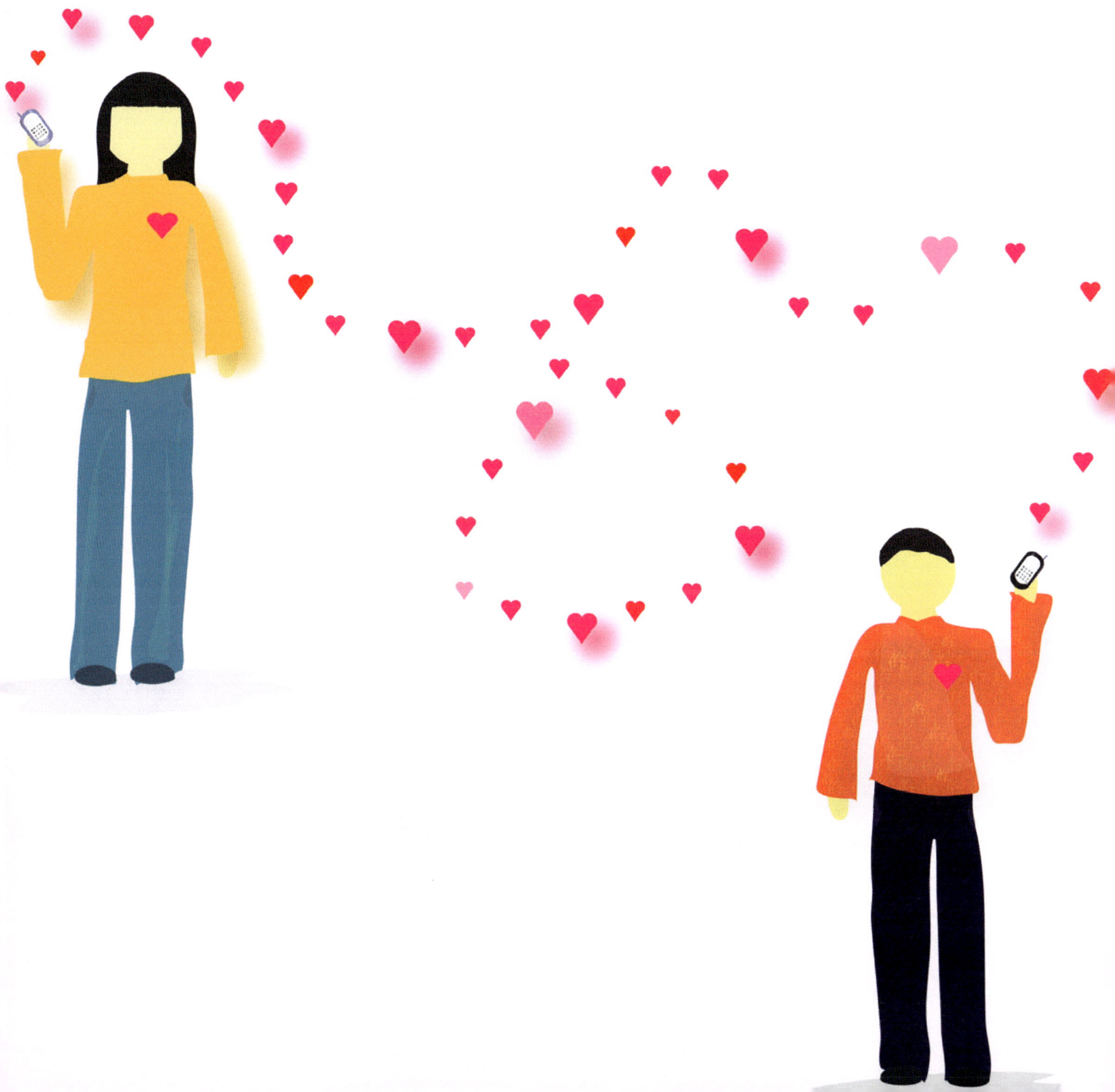

Families share their hopes and dreams together.
This family is dreaming about a fun trip and a dance show.
What is something your family would love to do together?

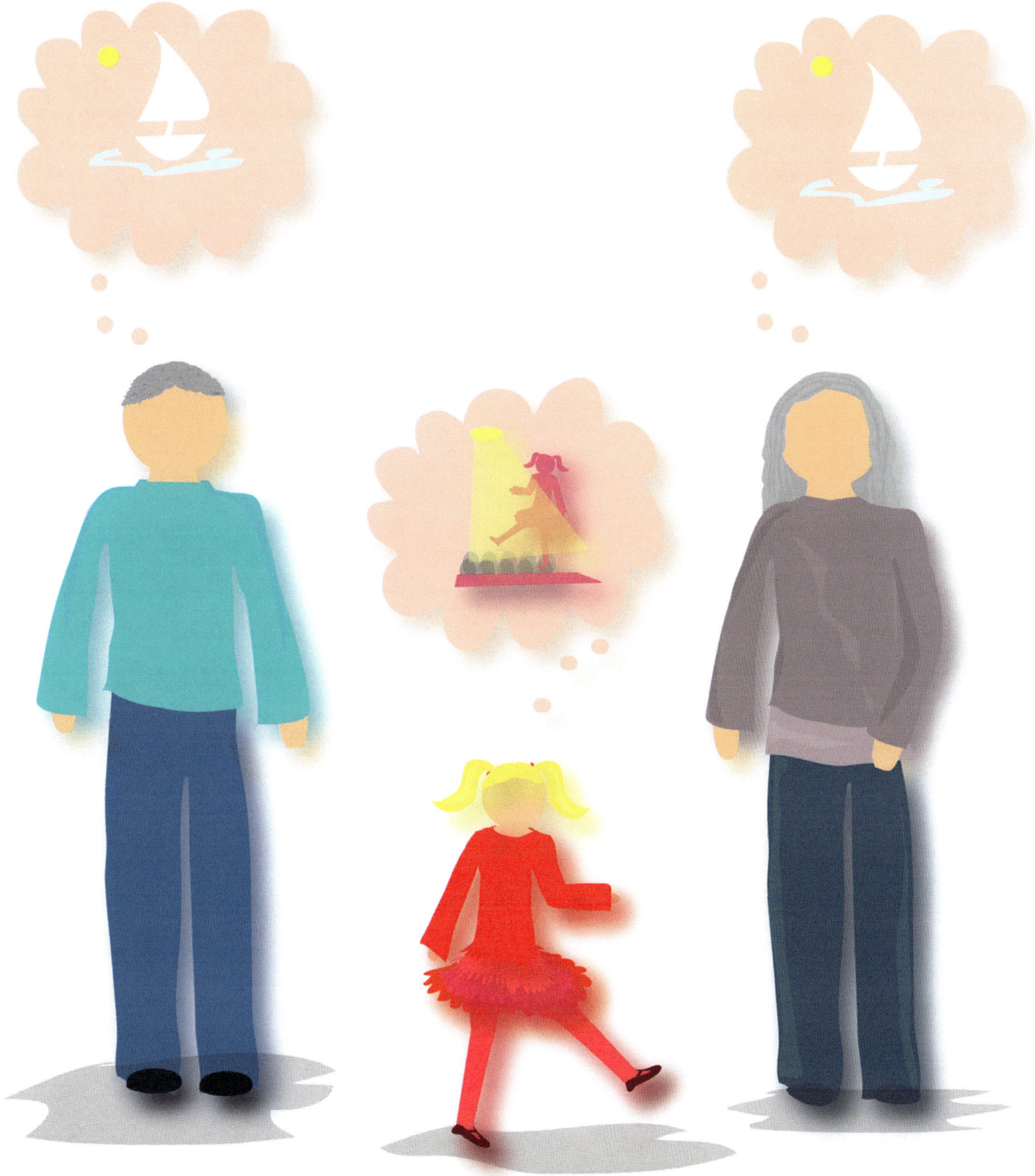

Now we know what a family is!

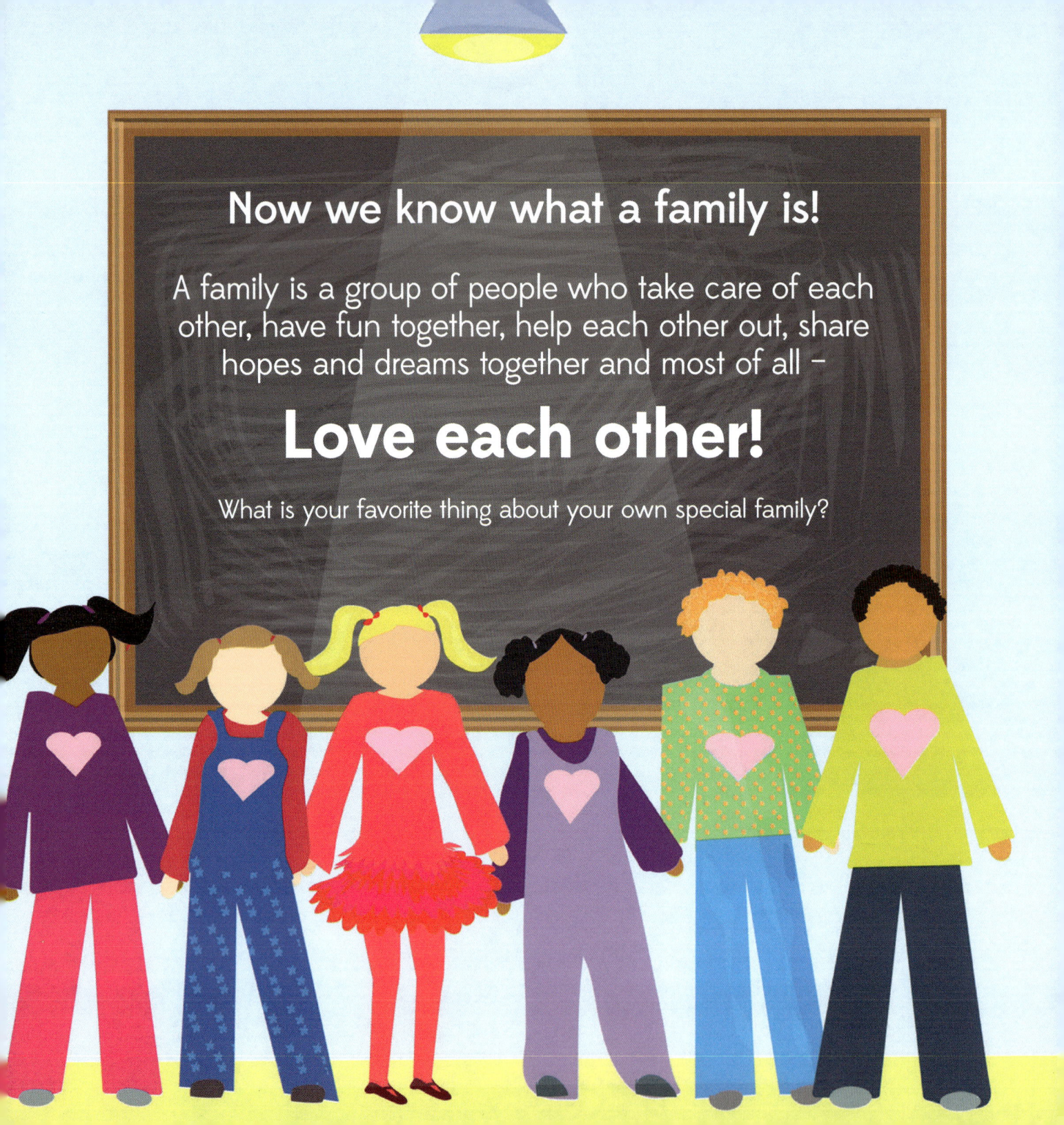

A family is a group of people who take care of each other, have fun together, help each other out, share hopes and dreams together and most of all −

Love each other!

What is your favorite thing about your own special family?

What does your special family look like?
Draw it on this page!

About the Author

Tamia Sheldon is a freelance illustrator and designer working outside of Seattle, WA.
She loves making up stories for her funny kid and spends all her free time drawing, reading and taking pictures.
With a B.A. in Design and Cultural Studies, she is intent on creating work that has a positive impact on the world.
Tamia the the author and illustrator of *The Hungry Shark* and *Let's Play* and the illustrator of *The Zebra Said Shhh* and *Toby the Flying Cat*.

Additional Books from Tamia

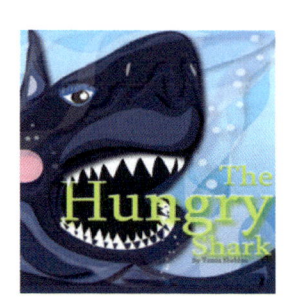

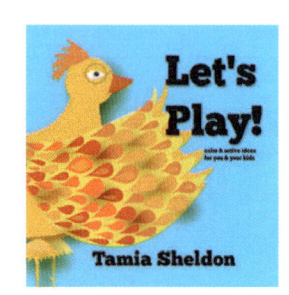

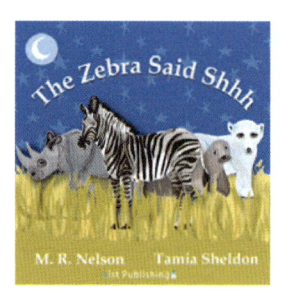

For Loving Families Everywhere

Copyright © Tamia Sheldon 2013
All Rights Reserved. No portion of this book may be reproduced without express permission from the publisher.

First Edition

ISBN-13: 9781623955274
eISBN: 9781623955281
ePIB ISBN: 9781623950569

Published in the United States by Xist Publishing
www.xistpublishing.com
PO Box 61593 Irvine, CA 92602